# IT'S TIME TO EAT LOGANBERRIES

# It's Time to Eat LOGANBERRIES

Walter the Educator

Silent King Books
A WhichHead Entertainment Imprint

Copyright © 2024 by Walter the Educator

All rights reserved. No part of this book may be reproduced in any manner whatsoever without written per- mission except in the case of brief quotations embodied in critical articles and reviews.

First Printing, 2024

Disclaimer

This book is a literary work; the story is not about specific persons, locations, situations, and/or circumstances unless mentioned in a historical context. Any resemblance to real persons, locations, situations, and/or circumstances is coincidental. This book is for entertainment and informational purposes only. The author and publisher offer this information without warranties expressed or implied. No matter the grounds, neither the author nor the publisher will be accountable for any losses, injuries, or other damages caused by the reader's use of this book. The use of this book acknowledges an understanding and acceptance of this disclaimer.

It's Time to Eat LOGANBERRIES is a collectible early learning book by Walter the Educator suitable for all ages belonging to Walter the Educator's Time to Eat Book Series. Collect more books at WaltertheEducator.com

**USE THE EXTRA SPACE TO TAKE NOTES AND DOCUMENT YOUR MEMORIES**

# LOGANBERRIES

It's time to eat, come gather near,

# It's Time to Eat
# Loganberries

A yummy treat is waiting here.

Red and juicy, sweet and tart,

Loganberries will warm your heart!

They grow on vines, so strong and green,

A hidden treasure, a snack supreme.

Pick them gently, soft and round,

A burst of flavor you have found!

Wash them clean with water's spray,

Now they're ready, hip hooray!

Put one in and take a bite,

Loganberries bring delight!

They taste like sunshine, wild and free,

A blend of raspberry and blackberry,

Soft and tangy, oh so sweet,

Loganberries are a perfect treat!

# It's Time to Eat
# Loganberries

Add them to your morning dish,

Yogurt, muffins, or a fruity wish.

Or eat them plain, just as they are,

Nature's candy, best by far!

Loganberries are good for you,

Full of vitamins and flavor too.

They keep you strong, they keep you bright,

A snack that makes you feel just right!

Let's thank the plants, so tall and grand,

For growing berries on the land.

With every bite, we smile and say,

"Thank you, berries, for this day!"

Share them with your family and friends,

The joy of berries never ends.

Pass the bowl and laugh with glee,

# It's Time to Eat
# Loganberries

Loganberries for you and me!

So next time when it's snack time fun,

Pick loganberries, one by one.

A fruity treat, so fresh and neat,

The perfect snack that's hard to beat!

Now let's all cheer, it's berry time,

A treat so simple, so sublime.

Loganberries, small and bright,

# It's Time to Eat
# Loganberries

Our favorite snack, morning or night!

# ABOUT THE CREATOR

Walter the Educator is one of the pseudonyms for Walter Anderson. Formally educated in Chemistry, Business, and Education, he is an educator, an author, a diverse entrepreneur, and he is the son of a disabled war veteran. "Walter the Educator" shares his time between educating and creating. He holds interests and owns several creative projects that entertain, enlighten, enhance, and educate, hoping to inspire and motivate you. Follow, find new works, and stay up to date with Walter the Educator™

**at WaltertheEducator.com**

www.ingramcontent.com/pod-product-compliance
Lightning Source LLC
LaVergne TN
LVHW052013060526
838201LV00059B/4005